To all who have loved
and embraced the cost of loving.

For Peggy McNabb

In sincere appreciation for
all your guidance & support.

Janis

May your
heart rejoice
in
love!

Bess

TABLE OF
Contents

$\mathcal{F}$oreword

It is better to have loved and lost than to have never loved at all—Alfred, Lord Tennyson, *In Memoriam*, 1850, line 27, stanza 4

As a talk show host for **WCCO** Radio, Brad Walton's intuitive, familiar voice is heard by thousands. He is best known for his quest for knowledge and meaning. His program has created a venue for politicians, authors, physicians, artists, and healers to convey their grandest thoughts and dreams.

His first book, *How Does The Heart Know Love?* is a sensitive and intimate collection of compositions, both prose and poetry, which explores his midlife journey following the death of his father, William, and friend, Al, and his own brush with death resulting in emergency open heart surgery.

The fact that these three experiences intersected Brad's life at midpoint seems, at first, a

1

strange coincidence. Many would have chosen bitterness or pity. Brad chose courage and sought to find meaning in his grief.

Healing is a mysterious process. Although physicians have documented its stages and phases, its source is still not understood. Healing seems to come from the body's own wisdom; health is a manifestation of balance, forgiveness, and love.

As the wound is repaired and the tissues grow strong, a scar is formed. With time, the wound and the scar become part of the whole…a reminder, a metaphor, a marker in time and place.

Brad Walton grapples with his pain the only way he knows, honestly, courageously, and head on. His story is eloquently told and painfully honest. It leaves the reader with a knowing—that we can, and do have the strength to heal, that we can survive tragedy and choose to love again and again…fearlessly.

Perhaps there is no such thing as coincidence.

Janis C. Amatuzio, M.D.
Midwest Forensic Pathology P.A.

Dr. Janis Amatuzio is a forensic pathologist, the appointed coroner for Anoka, Crow Wing, Meeker, Mille Lacs, and Wright counties, and president of Midwest Forensic Pathology, P.A. She is a frequently sought-out speaker/lecturer throughout the state. Her special interests are death investigation systems and insights into meaningful living. She is board certified in anatomic, clinical, and forensic pathology. In her book, *Forever Ours,* Dr. Amatuzio explores the mysterious realm of visions, experiences, and communications experienced by families at the threshold of the deaths of their loved ones. *www.foreverours.com*

THE WAY WE HEAL...
September 22, 1999

---

*And I will give you a new heart, and
put a new spirit into you; I will remove
the heart of stone from your body and
give you a heart of flesh.* Ezekiel 36:26

The changes that result from a pulsing universe at a crossroad of life and death are many. Our personal paradigms or epiphanies have a complex history with the relationships and events of our lives.

Prior to my heart attack on September 22, 1999, I had experienced the losses of my college roommate and best friend, Al, who was like a brother to me, and eighteen months later, my father, William, who was not only a parent but a friend. The uncharted journey of my grief related to their deaths was still fresh when I was confronted with my own mortality on that September evening.

Admitting to and facing my own chest pain on that evening was the beginning of my healing and an awakening that continues to this day.

Forty-five minutes after my chest pains began, I found myself in the very hospital where my friend Al had died three years earlier. My awareness of Al and this irony continued even in the vulnerable uncharted moments of lying on an emergency room table. I have reflected often on this irony of my admission and Al's life and death in that same setting.

I felt the pain of my struggling heart. It rolled and tightened, only finding relief with the medication given to keep it from going into full arrest. A series of tests were administered in the days that followed.

On September 24, I had an angiogram. Before I knew the test had started, it was over. The room went *silent!* After a few seconds of the bewilderment, I asked, "What's going on?" The reply, "Mr. Walton, you are going to have surgery on Monday!" My prognosis until that moment had been moving along on an optimistic note. In a matter of seconds, it became cautious and guarded.

Dr. Kit V. Arom, my surgeon, came to my room on Sunday morning. He wanted to review my angiogram and tell me about what he would be doing to my heart on Monday morning. It didn't look good. Before he left, I put my hand on his shoulder and asked him to do everything he could to bring me back if I arrested on the table. I wanted to say goodbye one more time to my friends and family. "Yes, I will!" he replied.

Monday morning on the way to surgery, I spoke my love and received the love of family and friends. The light inside the operating room was bright and the room was much colder than I had expected. The prayers I knew were many. I was cold and naked with an unknown outcome, yet I was at perfect peace. The last thing I remember is some laughter and conversation from those around the operating table.

Around 4:30 the next morning, in the early moments of my waking up and trying to move my hands and feet, I realized—for reasons of safety and protocol in ICU—that I had been strapped down. I panicked, gasping for air, and trying to reach for the tube I felt in my mouth. I was completely powerless. It was impossible even to gasp for air!

In the brief seconds that followed my panic, I quickly realized that to survive and live beyond this moment, I had to simply let go! The phrase *let go and let God* went through my mind. Only then could the tube intended to give me breath give me life.

Open heart surgery is in itself rich in metaphor. In both the physical and the spiritual worlds, our greatest pain comes at the time of our greatest healing. To think of my heart in the hands of those who could perform the healing art of heart surgery is not unlike the kind of understanding it takes to heal our wounded souls.

Had I not admitted, faced, and dealt with the pain I felt on that evening in September, I would not be alive today. I needed to admit to and feel my pain before and after surgery in order to heal. The way we heal is to let ourselves feel! My scars are a gift reminding me of the gift of love and life itself.

It is difficult to speak of how the heart feels or knows love. Yet the incredible pain of loving felt in this amazing organ bears testimony not only to the heart's profound design but to its meaning and purpose. The heart is the cradle of all that it means to be fully human.

What happened during surgery? I have no doubt that my soul was being reminded of what it was born to remember. Although all the words were not there following surgery, my awareness about life had changed. This surgery was not just a turning point but a transformation.

You will read much about pain and love in the following pages. There is a progression in the pages ahead. Each piece also stands by itself. You will find *italics* and *spaces* that are there for the sake of allowing you to *feel the words* and *breathe* the meanings in each page. Throughout this reading you will also encounter some repetition that is typical in this journey of the heart.

It was never my intention to write or publish these words. That which follows was simply written because I could do nothing else. I was compelled to write. Overwhelmed! The tears flowed and I felt my body shake. I knew this was about my transformation.

How we are changed and where those transformations take us is not as clear. There are those insidious changes that are almost negligible by themselves and then there are those ninety-degree turns. Both can transform us forever. Change is our one constant!

My surgery was the beginning of a personal and profound personal paradigm that still resonates with its ongoing lesson. The reality of a pulsing universe at a crossroad of life and death will change one in ways never anticipated in that moment of truth. If we are allowed to live beyond this moment of truth, we are given the gift of a second chance. I have been given that gift!

My heart at a *crossroad*—stopped and then started in the days following September 22, 1999—was soon to discover a language without words: deeper exchanges and lessons in matters of the heart too profound for words but rich with meanings seldom realized or spoken in love.

The cover of this book is rich with the symbolism that embraces both my journey and this book's title. My heart was put into the loving hands of the surgeon who would perform his healing art to give me life. When we choose to love, we put our hearts into the hands of another and receive theirs with ours. This is the sacred trust of life and love. We have the opportunity to learn much from the pain that comes from our loving. With love, our lessons can go even deeper; our healing can be more complete. We are forever changed by love.

It is always difficult to face our own pain. Love calls us to embrace its accompanying pain; the pain of its loving. Love honors its deepest expression and experience in this embrace. Love's eternal expression in this *finite* heart can do no less. Love knows its *eternal value* in a soul and between two souls. Love knows its *eternal* immeasurable imprint in this heart of flesh.

The pages of this book embrace my journey through many different types of loss. The thread common to all of them is about the love we give and receive in this life. These reflections also share my healing journey with those who have been there for me with their love, understanding, and presence.

May the reflections that follow be a resource for your life offering some insight into the probing question, *How does your heart know love?*

HOW PROFOUND IS THE

Human Heart?

You can fool your mind but not your heart!—**Author Unknown**

I am afraid to write. For if I write, I will feel. Feel deeply and *intensely*—but I can write in no other way. There is a depth of both heart and soul that is beyond measure, yet I know its depth.

Love is the superlative experience in our human journey. Love both calls and fulfills the essence of our humanity. So what does pain have to do with love? What does the embrace of our pain have to do with our healing and loving? What does grief have to do with healing?

We do not know or experience love's fullness until we complete the day filled with its seemingly antithetical contrasts. As light and darkness complete a day, so it is with love's light and essence, experienced in the darkness of our pain and grief. The shadows and silhouettes of the night are difficult to see and define, but they are so very present.

Oh, to go beyond the superficial and beyond pretense. To go beyond the traditional meanings and understandings and be willing to be profoundly vulnerable—deeply vulnerable—embracing the unknown in ways longed for but seldom realized. What does it mean to take the risk? Is not love like the thorn next to the exquisite rose?

Why do we run from the pain that comes from loving? To let ourselves feel pain is essential if we want to embrace, to honor, the love we've cherished. We shortchange love's essence and its completeness if we don't embrace its pain. Our heart feels the impact of our unspeakable pain in its greatest longing, love. That special person, pet, project, career, or place of devotion may no longer be in our present reality. But yet, it is and will be. Love's superlative song is sung in that moment of painful awareness.

Must the heart *break* before it discovers its essence? Is it like the seed that must die before it brings forth that for which it is created? Is it like the thorn bird that seeks the tree and the thorn it was created to embrace? Here is the beautiful introduction to Colleen McCullough's *The Thorn Birds*:

> "There is a legend about a bird, which sings just once in life, more sweetly than any other creature on the face of the earth. From the moment it leaves the nest it searches for a thorn tree, and does not rest until it has found one. Then, singing among the savage branches, it impales itself upon the longest, sharpest spine. And, dying, it rises above its own agony to out-carol the lark and the

10

nightingale. One superlative song, existence the price. But the whole world stills to listen, and God in His heaven smiles. For the best is only bought at the cost of great pain—Or so says the legend."

Love is the thorn of our creation. Our deepest longing is to be impaled through the heart by love. That is our superlative song and love's destiny. The pain of love's superlative song is also sung in the place where we feel our greatest pain, our heart. This is love's destiny—to impale from the time we are born.

We seek to love and be loved. But that also is what causes our unthinkable pain. Without love we die less than human; with it we feel pain never imagined. Yet it is that pain of loving that makes us fully human and fully alive. We honor love's essence when we embrace the pain of loving not as masochistic martyrs but as honorees of the gift of loving.

There is a stewardship of pain, the pain that comes from the loss and grief over that which we have loved. It is in our many losses that we discover new meanings otherwise never encountered. It is in the dark night of the soul where we give completeness to the experience of loving and being loved. Our need to embrace love's cost in order to heal is testimony to the significance and profound impact of love in this human heart.

The *tears* still come, though never before like this. They seem now to come from a deeper *spring*, a spring that I thought was covered. When tears come from the soul one only needs to follow the passion that comes from its *river*.

The soul's watershed moment is its *greatest affirmation*.

Death

Your pain is deep, and it won't just go away. It is also uniquely yours, because it is linked to some of your earliest life experiences. Your call is to bring that pain home. You have to incorporate your pain into your self and let it bear fruit in your heart and the hearts of others.—
Henri J. M. Nouwen

Now in this moment of unthinkable separation there is no recourse. Now is never again and forever changed.

Must my heart break before it discovers its essence? George C. Scott as *Scrooge* asks a similar question in his aloneness with these words, "What did I do to be abandoned like this?"

Death dictates no recourse for reunion. Sharing *presence* is no longer an option. The confrontation with my own mortality forces me to a new reality and a new awareness. The *finite* and the *eternal* meet here.

All of the possibilities of the past are no longer in the present or in the future. Any hope of reconciliation or reunion is now gone. No right words here. A new truth is telling me that I must be carried by something greater than the self, a self that no longer feels invincible.

Now the pain of the heart is like the bare trees of winter and the seed that seems lifeless but is very alive. I am forced to new meanings I would otherwise have never known or discovered. It is winter and my heart feels this cold separation. I see no new life coming from this cold ground. Have you ever wished you could stop your heart from feeling?

Tears are the water that birth new meaning in this lifeless moment. The pain in my heart in this new season of loss is about many things, but more than anything it is about moving me to feel and seek my healing. This is a time for presence with those I love and those who love me. A time for healing presence with those who also know the pain of the heart.

Death can never steal my profound love for another. Death can never take away the continuing relationship in all that love has given. My love does not die, but I feel unthinkable pain. Love's greatest enemy in this moment of grief is my unwillingness or inability to feel the pain of my loss.

A heart broken is not gone. My heart has simply, profoundly, become the seed that must die before its purpose is born.

THE LANGUAGE
of *Tears*

If I could come back as anything, it would be one of your tears. What more could I want than to be conceived in your heart, born in your eyes, live on your cheeks and die on your lips.—Source Unknown

---

There are but a few hidden teardrops we wear in the cost of loving. How do we say goodbye to love? Our hearts are not composed of paper or plastic to be thrown away or recycled. Our hearts are too fragile to be drawn close and then pushed away or ignored. For this love is like no other—it's too tender not to be answered. Transformed *forever*—this love never ends.

Now in this season of loss, love must find its way and place in a heart that is no longer answered. No more echoes of those unique connections that were shared in each other's presence.

Now in this silence, it is silence that must be embraced with only the memory of what was or could have been. The door has closed. Yet this heart is still so alive—tears are its language and its affirmation for that which will never die. Only the sound of its empty chambers echoes now.

I let myself cry! My healing does not come easy.

The deeper and richer meanings have begun their birth.

Pain is my teacher for this deeper language of the heart and soul. Tears are my heart's gift for that which can never be put into words. I must feel, speak, and write through my tears to redeem the pain.

Tears are the affirmation of love's reality. Tears are the soul's voice in a heart made alive by love.

LOVE'S SYMPHONIC
Composition

---

*The day will come when, after har-
nessing space, the winds, the tides and
gravitation, we shall harness for God
the energies of love. And on that day,
for the second time in the history of the
world, we shall have discovered fire.—*
**Pierre Teilhard de Chardin, French Palen-
tologist and Philosopher**

L ove is the superlative experience of our exis-
tence. It is the purpose of our design and
our humanity from the moment of our birth;
our deepest need and our greatest motivation,
in all of life is *to love* and *to be loved*. When it is
found, it is the source of both our greatest joy
and our greatest pain. Love and pain seem to
be antithetical to the human experience, but
one is essential to the efficacy of the other.

The pain of this love's absence is present
long before it is felt. The euphoria of love's
birth numbs us to the reality of the death that

eventually comes with this new life. This new life, this eternal life, is born loving forever and forever loved. The first verses of a lifetime of music are sung and shared when we are present but are played and remembered when there is no longer anyone to sing with us.

Love's pain must be honored in grief to be complete. Grief honors the pain of loving. Love's honor is born out of what is shared in presence and played in absence. The pain of hearing and remembering is embraced when presence is no more.

Here is love's completion. The full score has been written. The concert has been played. The superlative song now heard in silence, yet was never so fully orchestrated until now. Love's music is now heard in its completion. Its song is given back in the penetrating silence of our aloneness. Pain is its captive audience drawn to listen to every note and phrase. Music played! Listening is the healing embrace of that which we cannot speak.

Notes written, but now heard! The richness of love's meaning is expressed beyond words. The superlative of this love can only be felt; it is completed and put to music in its dying. Tears are the rain that keeps the soul from hardening.

Love's song, love's honor, is written with the pain that only love can know, the pain that only love can embrace.

BROKEN
Hearts

I was afraid of getting my heart broken again.—**The Pigeon Lady in** *Home Alone* 2

I s there a pain greater than that of a broken heart? Matters of the heart, both physical and spiritual, are superlative in every aspect of our person and journey. We often make the mistake of separating our physical heart from our soul. We often talk of broken hearts, but we seldom make the connection to that amazing rhythm inside each of us that it is more than just a pump moving blood through a human body.

The human heart is the stage for our journey, the centerpiece on which the drama of our souls is orchestrated and played. Here, feeling beyond emotion is felt at its deepest level. The best and most beautiful things in the world cannot be seen or even touched—*they must be felt with the heart.*

No character on this stage is more profound than love. No other experience in my human journey makes a more significant impact on my soul. With it I soar to my greatest heights and without it every part of me will die. It is in the experience of being loved and loving that I am made fully human and fully alive.

In the deep contrast of life and death, I am faced with what seems to be the antithetical contrast of that which I long for the most. I ask again, "Is love worth the price of its own pain?" It is in the face of many losses that I soon learn and am forced to deal with the cost of loving.

We often feel the pain of love's cost, but we don't know why. We don't understand that we feel the pain of our loving for good reasons. Pain is what teaches us about this language of the heart and soul, a language far beyond the spoken word, a language that must be felt to its completion. Here in the drama of the heart is where we find the deeper and richer meanings. We honor the gift of love by letting ourselves feel the pain that is at its essence.

Love is by its very nature the heart's superlative essence. To write or speak about this pain of loving is both redemptive and difficult. This completion of love's honor and essence does not come easily. Love's fullness is known only by its unmistakable price.

LOVE: THE INDELIBLE *Mystery*

> *...recognize and embrace your unique suffering. You have to live through your pain gradually and thus deprive it of its power over you.*—Henri J. M. Nouwen

L ove is the most profound word in any language for it is the universal language of the heart. This indelible mystery of love and suffering is a gift to be lived. There is a knowing and a defining moment in this deep grief. It knows a value that cannot and will never be measured or replaced.

The heart can know beyond all doubt the gift of this loving, a profound life-changing depth. Significance and meaning that are unique to a lifetime with a heart that is willing to feel the corners that it has never felt or known before now. This love embraces the whole heart. This heart's new awareness has awakened to the heart of the other; it has found not only itself but its other half.

Love embraces the life-giving paradox of embracing another kindred heart completely without losing itself. The heart can be completely given away but never diminished. The heart is found in its giving—*totally vulnerable*, yet without fear. The heart's essence is realized without pretense or condition.

I must not be afraid to feel my loss and continue loving that one who is no longer present, for love's loving is *forever*. I honor this love by letting myself feel their absence, embracing it with tears, and forever holding dear the privilege I have had in this meeting and this knowing. What a unique and profound privilege of sacred trust when holding another's heart! It was Elizabeth Kubler-Ross who said, "If we dare to love—we must have the courage to grieve."

I must let this fragile heart in this mortal body embrace my eternal connection with another soul. That is what completes and honors something that cannot be spoken.

The *infinite* is now embraced by the *finite!*

HOW DOES THE
Heart Know Love?
I

We embrace love's pain because it is also the true experience of love and the lover. By the time our heart is aware of love's transforming power, it has already been captured by love's essence; it is destined to know its unmistakable thorn. This is love's redemptive cost. To run from or deny it is to deny our hearts the beauty of love itself. We cannot live without love, but the pain of true love is inevitable. We are called to honor and complete that which we have longed for—**love**.

Our fear of the thorns should not keep us from the rose. There is no way around the pain of loving and being loved. I, like the thorn bird, impale myself on the very thing I cannot live without; to live without it, I stop living. How can I look into the mirror and forget the eyes that embrace my soul? How do I run from my own soul and the kiss that it has felt?

Deep territory! No regrets for meeting, for loving and being loved. Love becoming aware of the value and meaning of pain. The pain still present is now redemptive.

What does pain have to do with my healing? It is in the embrace of my pain that I honor the gift of loving. I honor and give purpose to my grief. My healing begins. New meanings take form.

Grief is the journey of honoring all that my love has embraced, of discovering meanings never known or understood until I have walked in such darkness. These are the colors and images of the night never seen during the day. Grief is the supreme affirmation of love's embrace in this mortal heart. The late author M. Scott Peck wrote, "To love much is also to feel much pain."

How does the heart know love? The heart knows love when I am willing to speak and feel, "I love you enough to let myself feel the pain my heart will know in your absence." A heart willing to feel the pain of absence is a heart that still knows and affirms the joy of loving in life and in death.

Love's affirming distinction is felt in the spirit, and its measure is known by the soul. Love's cost is redeemed with its own tears. Love's honor is realized in a heart forever changed.

Love's eternal imprint continues in this beating heart of flesh!

A HEART
of Flesh

...and give you a heart of flesh.—
Ezekiel 36:26

The heart is far more than four muscular chambers moving blood to every part of our body. Its essence is, as author Gary Zukav says, *the seat of the soul.* That essence is experienced and embraced not only by its amazing design and rhythm, both seen and felt, but by the overwhelming unseen energy that flows from this organ. Like the air we breathe, it is this unseen aspect of this heart of flesh that we so often neglect in our understanding.

We feel the pain of a broken heart but don't understand why. We find it difficult to accept the fact that we feel pain for good reasons. Those reasons are becoming more evident as modern research provides greater insight into this incredible organ. The physical and the spiritual worlds are joined here. In the average lifetime, the heart beats 2.5 billion times. The heart pumps about 1 million barrels of blood during an average lifetime—enough to fill more than three supertankers.

In recent years, scientists have discovered new information about the heart that has made them realize it's far more complex than any of us had imagined. There is new scientific evidence that the heart sends us emotional and intuitive signals to help govern our lives. Instead of simply pumping blood, scientists have discovered that the heart directs and aligns many systems in the body so they can function in harmony with each other. While the heart is in constant communication with the brain, scientists now know that it also makes many of its own decisions!

The heart is the most powerful generator of electromagnetic energy in the human body, producing the largest rhythmic electromagnetic field of any of the body's organs. The heart's electrical field is about 60 times greater in amplitude than the electrical activity generated by the *brain*. This field, measured in the form of an electrocardiogram (ECG), can be detected anywhere on the surface of the body.

Modern research has revealed and documented that the magnetic field produced by the heart is more than 5,000 times greater in strength than is the field generated by the brain, and can be detected a number of feet away from the body, in all directions, by using SQUID-based magnetometers.

New findings by those working with the HeartMath Group have found that the cardiac field is modulated by different emotional states. The group has performed several studies to investigate the possibility that the electromagnetic field generated by the heart may transmit information that can be received by others. The heart's electromagnetic field—by far the most powerful rhythmic field produced by the human body—not only envelops every cell of the body but also extends out into all directions in the space around us.

Even when we are not consciously communicating with others, our physiological systems interact in subtle and surprising ways. Did you know that the electromagnetic signal produced by your heart is registered in the brain waves of people around you? Or that your physiological responses sync up with your mate's during empathetic interactions?

There are three main power tools of the heart—love and appreciation, nonjudgement, and forgiveness. Every core heart feeling is a potential power tool—compassion, patience, and courage to name a few. Key to all of them is sincerity.

Dr. Rollin McCraty of the HeartMath Research Center and Institute of HeartMath says, "I believe that the electromagnetic energy generated by the heart is an untapped resource within the human system awaiting further exploration and application. Acting as a synchronizing force within the body, a key carrier of emotional information, and an apparent mediator of a type of subtle electromagnetic communication between people, the cardiac bioelectromagnetic field may have much to teach us about the inner dynamics of health and disease as well as our interactions with others."

For centuries, poets and philosophers have sensed that the heart is at the center of our lives. Saint-Exupéry wrote,

"And now here is my secret, a very simple secret: it is only with the heart that one can see rightly; what is essential is invisible to the eye."

Modern medical science and research now responsibly affirm that this pulsing universe is a key mediator of energetic interactions, emotional information, and communication between people.

PRESENCE AND LISTENING

the Heart is Heard

Life is not a problem to be solved, but a mystery to be lived.—**M. Scott Peck**

Oh, for this amazing heart to be heard! Now there is someone to listen. The gift of this listening affirms a knowing of both heart and soul. As the heart knows love and the soul knows connection, so both know the profound measure and the distinction of what cannot be measured. Sometimes the soul encounters a love, a connection to someone so profound, an experience so unique; it wonders if it is real. This meeting is like no other.

"All real living is meeting," said Martin Buber. Meeting is an art. There are those encounters and those meetings so loving that they completely transform us. The healing results that come from someone who truly listens permeate every chamber of our heart.

The awakened heart now hears the echoes of our soul that have been *silenced* or no longer heard or never before spoken. Chambers of our heart we never knew existed or chambers that have gone to sleep are now alive. We experience new and healing awareness that shows us what we have never been or will be until we embrace this new love, this kindred spirit, this mirrored soul remaining unique to its own identity.

The heart knows a value beyond any measure or comparison. It knows a meaning in time that embraces both its present and eternal value. It knows and nurtures the deep communion of the spoken and the unspoken.

The supreme exchange comes through the connection of our souls, and for that, there are no words. It is a mystery mutually understood, knowing it will never fully understand. We accept and live this mystery as a gift. We celebrate this mystery with unspoken awe in the silence of an embrace through our eyes, the window of the soul, and through the silent encounter of two souls as one.

A PULSING UNIVERSE

Awakened

…love is the willingness to extend one's self for the purpose of nurturing one's own or another's spiritual growth.—M. Scott Peck

---

Someone has heard and taken the time to listen! This awakened heart now has a clarity that occurs when kindred hearts meet and then share presence. That is when a new reality is met on all levels, a synchronicity beyond words. Let us always find a way to meet and share that eternal moment in finite time. For this shared presence has unlocked a deep spring that now flows within.

In my weakest moments and my greatest tears, I feel strong with you. My heart is now confident enough to fumble, to be silent and awkward. That is true love. The words I must speak will only come with the gift of your presence. Then this gentle stream, this mighty river, has a place to flow. Its churning has purpose.

The *silent roar* of this pulsing universe has awakened to a distinctive transcendent language. Its beauty fills the spirit with awe, with wonder only imagined but never thought possible.

How profound is the human heart? There inside a finite space is an eternal space for you—flesh beating, rhythm dancing, connecting body and soul. This heart has now encountered an intimate awareness of its own eternity and yet, simultaneously it is aware of its mortal vulnerability. Vulnerable in love, this pulsing universe awakens with the *light* of your presence. Be my friend forever! Let us embrace the inexpressible gift of what we have awakened in each other and ourselves.

You, like no other, draw from the deepest well. A thirst is born, a well is drawn, a thirst is quenched in the wonder of you.

THE EAGLE

Soars...

The eagle *soars* on currents unseen.

Its wings embrace and are embraced.
Giving flight!
Freed to fly...
to know a *freedom* that comes in its soaring.

Created to soar!
The eagle like no other
flies in the storm.

Your love is *like no other*.

Have our wings not endured the strongest of tests?
Has our flight not endured the greatest of storms?

We have taken the risk of not only flight
and know the majesty of flying together;
our wings complimenting the currents of the other.

And now we know a grace otherwise unknown.
We know an immeasurable height.
Height, not measured by how far we fly
    from the ground
but in our freedom to soar.

HOW DOES THE HEART KNOW LOVE?

When I rest, my heart still soars!
For we have flown together in a journey rarely taken.
Heights embraced at each other's side.
Wings fully spread.

Ours the gift of a *kindred eternal flight!*

© 2004 Brad Walton

LOVING
Presence

---

*Deeper than any level of dialog is the enjoy-
ment of another person.*—Gerhard Frost

Nothing is more profound in our human
experience than the *unconditional* loving
presence of another human heart. This pres-
ence validates beyond any spoken word. Here
beyond the spoken is spirit, heart, and soul.
Here, in a totally different dimension, we are
bonded by a loving communion distinct with
its unspoken reciprocity. Loving presence is
the gift of the interplay and the exchange of
two hearts. How is it that this shared pres-
ence answers the profound depth known and
embraced in the unspoken conversation? What
is the unique and profound answer our souls
exchange when in each other's presence?

Unconditional love is present when the
heart is drawn to listen deeply and to hear the
conversation of the soul. Words and meanings

flow in deep and powerful moments of awareness. A transformation is *realized* when unconditional love is answered in kind.

How can another be so positively profound?

My humanity finds its deepest meaning and expression in the presence of another kindred loving heart. Nothing in my human experience is more profound. The presence of another so profound that even before I experience the absence of that kindred soul, I am aware of the contrast that I will experience with their absence. This awareness comes even before their *absence* is a reality. My soul instinctively knows how absence defines the deafening moments of my aloneness.

Absence is known and felt because of presence. The depth and significance of presence is not known until we embrace the experience and the pain of absence through separation. The intensity of our grief flows in direct proportion to the strength and power of those rich meanings and the purpose we shared in presence.

The superlative absence without recourse is death. Being present is no more, but our *relationship continues*. The indelible imprint shared in love is forever with me. Presence does not leave me. This new experience of presence, too holy to describe, can only be honored when I take the time to *feel the pain* of the absence.

In our grief and loss we are moved to define this new presence. This indelible imprint on our souls now needs a new chapter and a witness to this new writing—someone to hear us read about a new reality we could have never imagined. The birth of this new reality is validated with the presence of that kindred soul, who will listen not only with ears, but with heart and spirit. It is the sacred trust of listening, knowing, believing, and loving.

Our tendency is to go it alone, to tough it out, to survive. We develop an inner cynicism that we repeat to ourselves in silent ways—that no one will care enough to really listen and understand. But the gutsy and deep issues of our lives need the ear and presence of someone who truly loves us for who we really are and where we are at in that moment—*unconditionally!* Our healing comes with a life-giving language that is beyond the spoken word but known in the heart.

LIFE GIVING
Language

---

the lifegiving
language
of love.
its firm
resounding
affirmation
of living…
embracing life itself.

knowing
a depth
it has never known…
in its knowing.
one that cannot be measured
or compared…
but *incomparably* felt
and known.

for you inspire
a depth
and a knowing
that comes from an untapped
well.

one ready to flow
with voiceless words
and meanings.

insights newly expressed
with a deeper clarity,
unique…
but *universal*…
to the power of love
and loving.

a meeting of two hearts
and souls.

in the mystery of that meeting
two experience
a connection…
that opens a *wellspring*
of expression…
to enlighten
and bring
understanding
unique to their *union* and yet
universal to the experience of love.

© 2004 Brad Walton

HEALING
Presence

> It is through the pain of confronting and
> resolving problems that we learn.—**M.**
> **Scott Peck**

ealing presence is simply being in the
presence of someone who really cares.
Tears and silence are a beautiful affirmation
of true presence. Even more so when we have
come from a place where we have been hurt
or wounded. Presence is, I believe, the way
we find our way back and discover our path to
healing. Matters of the heart are superlative!
We long for that healing presence. In the *light*
of their love, we feel the safety necessary to
do our emotional and spiritual homework. Isak
Dinesen in her work *Out of Africa* writes, "All
sorrows can be borne if you can put them into
a story or tell a story about them."

It is time to let ourselves feel our pain. In
our deepest moments of pain, we discover

the undiscovered parts of our own heart and soul. This is the beginning of a profound awakening. Through pain, a deeper knowing about love occurs. We must feel through that which is inexpressible before we can even begin to express the words we need to share. This new depth of heart brings a knowing that gives us a way to speak. Words and meanings begin to flow in deep and powerful realizations and awareness. Our hearts will experience that kindred language spoken without words.

A loving presence will change us in ways never imagined, bringing healing and meanings found with no one else. Few understand or take the time to be present with such love, to be willing to listen as our soul speaks its pain. When we meet that kindred soul who listens unconditionally to the deepest part of our soul, the new meanings emerge.

One of the mysteries of love in this universe is when two hearts hear and express the pain and joy in the voice of each other's soul. New meanings are born from this mystery of a healing communion. New truths become a part of us when another takes the time to listen to our heart with theirs. Healing occurs when that kindred spirit and soul answers in kind, in the simplicity of just being present.

The pain in our heart is about many things, but more than anything it is about moving us to seek the healing of those we love and who also know love's pain of the heart. There is an immeasurable depth in the shared understanding and the silent communion of these two souls. Few aspects in the experience of our healing are more significant than the deep affirmation we experience in the embrace of a healing presence.

POETRY OF THE
Heart

two wings
embracing the unseen
held by the unseen
lifted by what they cannot see
soaring because of what they feel
yes, *lifted*
by its real presence
able to *soar…*
in ways like never before
to places
and to heights
unexplored.

there is a poetry of the heart
and you are the inspiration for
all its *words* and *meanings*.

© 2004 Brad Walton

BEYOND WORDS
Silent Communion

Silence first makes us pilgrims. Secondly, silence guards the fire within. Thirdly, silence teaches us how to speak.—Henri J. M. Nouwen

It is *silence* born from *solitude* that frees us to hear this new heart.

Words will never be complete enough to express our deepest, most profound *feelings*. Beyond love and emotion lies something deeper—something felt, known, and honored only in silence. Silence is a rare and treasured gift to this healing heart!

Moments of silence now bring that distinctive encounter between heart and soul.

In this meeting is a voice that speaks in the *silence*. Only in silence can I hear and honor this voice—a kindred union, affirming my heart is more than flesh—a warm beating flesh where the soul itself is seated and experienced.

Only in stillness can I listen to this heart beat and hear its voice. The moment of truth comes in listening, not speaking, in feeling the new and deeper meanings spoken in this moment of silence.

This moment of silence has been forever spoken. Indelible is its imprint on my soul!

One of those moments in time that will resonate forever. No need for words.

Silence!

SOULS

Dancing

a million words could never replace
the honor and truth of what can *only be felt*.

that one can describe love's beauty
but to honor its essence
one must *feel* it.

souls dancing...

this the *silent dance*
like the *light* of the stars we embrace.

only the heart can embrace
the *splendor* of this light.

solitude speaks the eternal
in that *tender* moment...

a new language *resonates*
a call to *listen* to this new voice...

we speak in this *silence...*

with a heart *willing* to feel
the completion of love's *superlative song!*

HOW DOES THE
Heart Know Love?
II

...the greatest of these is love. —**The Apostle Paul to the Corinthians**

L ove is what gives birth to the reality of that embrace which cannot be measured or quantified in the kindred connection of two souls. This meeting gives birth to new words and feelings, conceived and born into this pulsing cradle of flesh. It is that profound. The shared tears of loving are a gift. They flow freely in the presence and safety of this soul's light. Vulnerable again, the heart finds its healing. The cost of loving finds its redemption. Love is our essence if only we can embrace it.

How does the heart know love? More sure than anything else in all the universe is the experience of love. And the heart does know love and the soul knows not only the moment but the depth of and significance of this connection. In one of his many writings, author Gerhard Frost reminds us, "Deeper than any level of dialog is the enjoyment of another person." The unexpected gift of this experience is too significant to ignore. The soul's passion is born from this kindred connection.

This profound experience calls us to see ourselves from the eyes of the beloved. It calls us to see me through you and you through me. And as we do, we hold each other's heart as the most precious thing our hands will ever touch. We hold each other's heart as a sacred trust beyond words, as the essence of all it means to be fully human ... fully alive ... fully embraced. We love another so completely that we put our hearts in the hands of the other and look into their eyes, the window of their soul. This act is a sacred trust of the *heart*.

The heart knows love when no words need be spoken. A warm embrace and the eyes of another speak more than words could give justice to. We can speak when all the words are there; we can know and embrace the *silence* when the words are not. When our mouths are closed and our ears hear *silence*, our souls will listen and speak.

It was Carl Jung who said, "The meeting of two personalities is like the contact of two chemical substances; if there is any reaction, both are transformed." And that applies to this unsought gift of meeting and loving. Our finite moments are given freely to discover the eternal!

How precious the soul who chooses to embrace the cost of loving and to commit to such a journey! That discovery is ours if we embrace it. May we so treasure the gift of loving and all it embraces that we never disregard our heart's most precious gift.

Oh, to be so free to speak the eternal words that say it all, *"I LOVE YOU!"*

THE CHOIR AWAKENED

Now Sings

after the rain
as the sky clears,
the birds begin to sing
in that amazing choir.

I love this choir!

the best and most beautiful things in the world
cannot be seen or even touched—
they must be *felt with the heart.*

...and I feel you...

my heart sings with those birds
in that morning light.

I look out...
and *smell*...not only the fresh air...
but the gentle *soft*...pine.

I *feel* the wind
whispering through the pines.

oh the accents of this *majestic* choir
singing their *eternal* chorus.

HOW DOES THE HEART KNOW LOVE?

each their own song
but all together...a *transcendent* harmony.

together...
they create...
a *symphony*...
a masterpiece...
unique to the day...
and to the moment...
they are *embraced*...
by those who take the time to *feel* and *listen*.

FEAR

Not

If we dare to love—we must have the courage to grieve.——**Elizabeth Kubler-Ross**

They that sow in tears shall reap in joy.——**Psalm 126:5**

In the first chapter I shared my story about two very significant losses in my life. I remember in my early days of grief following the death of my friend Al and later, my father, William, being confronted with the difficult choice of whether to remove or keep their pictures on my desk. My choice to keep their pictures in front of me every day since their passing has been one of the most difficult but healing choices in my journey of grief. I often feel a sense of their presence that still brings both comfort and tears. My memory fills with the joy of the times we shared. The inspiration of their lives inspires my life today with a richness I would never have known had I not chosen to keep those pictures on my desk and let myself feel the pain of their absence. This is the eternal song of the love we shared that continues in my life today.

Facing my own pain and mortality was also the catalyst for my healing. The significance of love's gift to this mortal heart might be best understood through a dialog in the final scene of *City of Angels* between an angel and a former angel who gave up immortality for the brief but profound experience of love. *If you had the choice to go back and do it all over again, would you?* The former angel responds, *I would rather have had one breath of her hair, one kiss from her mouth, one touch of her hand, than eternity without it.*

This amazing heart knows love's eternal imprint, because its purpose and complex design is what gives us the ability to know love and also honor the inevitable pain that comes in times of loss. I would not know or feel love without this beautiful heart!

There is a deeper knowing of the heart and soul that comes from the experience of love. I am convinced that the pain we feel in the experience of our loving, although at times beyond what we can or could imagine, can and will transform us into something better, with deeper meaning.

Even today, my own survival is not a result of something I could have done by myself. My healing has come as a result of the unconditional loving presence of those who have taken the time to listen to my broken heart. This awakened heart has experienced a healing, the gift of other kindred hearts willing to take the risk of sharing their heart and truly knowing mine. *Love brought me back!*

That which my heart knows it continues to embrace.

SUGGESTED REFERENCES

with Credits

Forever Ours, Dr. Janis Amatuzio, *www.foreverours. com*

As I Journey On (Meditations for those Facing Death), Sharon Dardis and Cindy Rogers, Augsburg Fortress

The Road Less Traveled, M. Scott Peck, Touchstone Books

Further Along the Road Less Traveled, M. Scott Peck, Touchstone Books

Can You Drink the Cup?, Henri J. M. Nouwen, Ave Maria Press

The Thorn Birds, Colleen McCullough, Avon Books

Journey to the Heart, Melody Beattie, Harper Collins

Color of the Night, Gerhard Frost, Augsburg Fortress

Heart-Brain Neurodynamics: The Making of Emotions, Dr. Rollin McCraty, *www.heartmath.org*

The Energetic Heart: Bioelectromagnetic Interactions Within and Between People, Dr. Rollin McCraty, *www.heartmath.org*

The HearthMath Solution—Doc Childre and Howard Martin with Donna Beech, *www.heartmath.org*

Science of the Heart—HeartMath Research Center, *www.heartmath.org*

On Death and Dying, Elizabeth Kubler-Ross, Scribner; Reprint

SUGGESTED VIEWING

Out of Africa, 1985 Universal Pictures

City of Angels, 1998 Warner Studios

Home Alone 2: Lost in New York, 1992 Warner Studios

SUGGESTED LISTENING

Streams—WORD Entertainment

Acknowledgements

Dr. Kit V. Arom, Dr. Michael Garr, Dr. Spencer Johnson, Dr. Jan Johnson, and Dr. Brenda Hurtt for your love and excellence in the healing art of medicine; to every nurse at St. John and St. Joseph's Hospital (*each one of you is an angel!*); Dr. Janis Amatuzio for her compassionate support, guidance and insight; the loving memory of Dr. Jonathan H. Kvernen; Dr. Janice Winchester-Nadeau for helping me understand the dynamics of loss and grief; Milt Adams of Beaver's Pond Press for his leadership and diligence as a most wonderful mentor; Jaana Bykonich and Jack Caravela at Mori Studio for their outstanding graphic sensitivities; Cindy Rogers for her editing excellence; back cover photo, Natalie Anderson; proofreading by Terri Hudoba; Suzanna Stickney, Galen Southard, Taylor Lynne Smith, and Bill Pearce for their encouragement to publish, Robert C. H. Parker for his compassionate counsel and spiritual guidance, the loving memory and friendship of Alan Sansgaard, the loving memory and friendship of my father William Walton; the love and support of my mother Marlene Walton; the loving support of my family—Marlene, Sharalee, David, and my friends—Dan, Keith, David, Rich, Danielle, Pastor Bob, Echo, Melody, Nancy, Kathy, and Jennifer; and finally the wonderful staff and listeners of **WCCO** Radio.

I love you—each and every one!

CONTACT INFORMATION

For speaking engagements, permissions, or to share your personal story contact Brad at:

howdoestheheart@yahoo.com

www.howdoestheheart.com